# CHASING SHEEP

## 8 VITAL TOPICS FOR THOSE CONSIDERING PASTORAL MINISTRY

Christopher J. Weeks

# Initial Thoughts

"Followers want comfort, stability, and solutions from their leaders, but that is babysitting. Real leaders ask hard questions and knock people out of their comfort zones and then manage the resulting distress."
*Harvard Business Review*

As the pastor of a growing church, I have been approached by a number of people asking me the same question in a number of different ways, "How does a person know if they are called into ministry? How do you know if you should be a pastor of a church?" Is it just another career choice alongside being a butcher, baker, or candlestick maker? Well, things have changed a bit, so it is more like being asked to compare yourself to becoming a broker, code writer, or barrister at a local coffee shop.

Since I have been serving in the church in the capacity of lead pastor for almost 25 years, I have wrestled with this question a lot. I sometimes wake up in a cold sweat haunted by my decision to serve Christ as a shepherd, wondering if I have opted for the easiest path, but then realizing at times my choice turned out to be the most treacherous and the rockiest trail of all. Hearing God's call is one of those subjects that is hard to really nail down. In fact, more than once I have asked myself in the heat of battle, "Have I really been specifically chosen by God to do this? Because I am not having fun right now."

"Calling" is an intensely subjective term. It means many different things to many different people. For some it is a feeling. For others, it is an obvious anointing that when exercised there is tangible proof that your gifts really do bless others. But for so many, "calling" is a vague misty idea, like a whisper in the wind — which is nearly impossible to grasp. So to help find some solid answers, I decided to write this devotional booklet that addresses different ways to consider how to approach the certainty of having a calling. Working in the front lines of a local church that ministers to up to 1,000 souls can be quite hazardous and exhausting. Mine is a curious congregation where people are often sick and sometimes dying, where someone is sure to be offended by another member and leaves, or a certain group is always questioning your sermons, your vision or choice of color on the auditorium walls, making pastoring incredibly frustrating. For those of you who are seeking to go into the full-time service of Jesus, it is first necessary to know if you are actually "called".

So these ideas come from the trenches — sharing what I have learned from personal experience and talking with those who have also served in the smoke and gunfire of real ministry. My humble thoughts are placed on paper for the purpose of helping a person who wants to know if they are actually called. Hopefully, this will be a great resource for those of you who have wondered, like me, if God may be calling you to serve him with your life. The most incredible and wild ride a man could ever imagine.

## Setting the Stage

The opinions I share in these pages are not derived from textbooks, or seminary classes — they are insights from working face-to-face with sinners and saints. Pastoring is not for the timid, and the initial sparkle and shine from mounting the pulpit for the first Sunday at your new church fades fast because the brokenness of life, like water pouring through a gaping leak, cannot be stopped. As Eugene Peterson once said, "Two things are true about every congregation: Everyone in the church is a sinner, and so are you as their pastor." Pastoring is more than preaching, it is learning to love God's dear people.

I must admit I am becoming more post-modern every day. I have found that life doesn't follow hard-edged plans or how-to guidelines that fit nicely on an alliterated outline. Navigating through the ups-and-downs of serving Christ is more like sailing a ship on a rough ocean; it takes perseverance, honesty, and God's gracious speed. So before we begin this study you must be ready to be brutally honest with yourself, and go below the surface of mere niceties and sentimentalism. Mere hype and false hope have shipwrecked many a green-horned dreamer hoping for glory and fame in a war-torn land. Personally, when it comes to being real, I want the bloody red meat, the human feel of an issue. Grab my soul, and give me the gut-wrenching truth. That, my dear reader, will be my objective with this study.

So get ready to probe and take your time meditating on what you really think because this is a "calling" where you will be forced to wrestle with God. And wrestling with God is a very dark and dangerous endeavor. Once he grabs you in a scissor hold he will squeeze tight and won't let go until you become the man he wants you to be — just ask Jacob (Genesis 32:22-30).

In truth, serving Jesus is not a job, it really isn't — it is an honor! There are eight areas that we will address, and I believe they are the issues you cannot ignore if you are going to have a ministry that pleases him:

- Guarding Your Heart
- Feeding Your Mind

- Navigating Your Family
- Maintaining a Devotional Life
- How to View Christ's Bride....the Church
- Mastering Speech
- Fostering the Habit of Rest
- Dealing With the Urgent

If you ignore any of these eight areas, destruction is certain — either in your life or the body of believers that you have been assigned to love. So before we journey on this muddy, narrow and rocky road, you must ask yourself this simple opening question;

*Is there anything else in life that excites you as much as a career or calling in ministry?*

If the answer is yes, you must first pursue that path. You must! If you don't, when the going gets tough, and mind you it will get tough, the residue of regret can kill your ministry when you are in the trenches. The ankle-deep mud in the trenches is real and it is smelly, so don't let the "could have been" or "should have been" regrets embitter your soul. Take your time on thinking through that initial question and if you are ready, we will begin.

# 1

# Guarding Your Heart

"Watch over your heart with all diligence,
for from it flows the springs of life."
*Proverbs 4:23*

If you lose your heart you lose your ministry. Who
wants to follow somebody that is a dead shell, a man
with no pulse? Who wants to worship with a cold
person who is doing everything just to get a paycheck?
Far too many servants of the living God are in the
ministry only to serve themselves, and the poor sheep
are suffering for it. Many a treasure hunting troll has
been lured into the ministry because they are told it is
rewarding, there is a pot of pure gold at the end of a
glory rainbow where you can grab for yourself a great
title and position, plus you really only work one day a
week... right?

That is the irony of this job, it isn't a job. It is a
journey across a wild ocean of rolling waves and

dangerous shoals. It is hard to say if it is a definite "calling" either, where some believe the voice of God audibly speaks to you and tells you exactly where to go (which I am still waiting to hear). Many people have their own stories and would argue with me on that point, but in my experience, I am convinced pastoring is first and foremost a

\* FIRM \* SURE \* & \* PASSIONATE \*

belief that God alone is true and every man a liar. Jesus himself said that most men only want the glory that comes from others. But to hold out for God's glory alone takes extreme patience and dedication. This bold mindset can only come from a spiritually healthy heart. According to scripture, the heart is the innermost engine of the soul that controls everything else in your life (Acts 13:22). If your heart is healthy, your ministry will be healthy. If your heart is sick, people will suffer.

I have three questions to gauge just how healthy your heart is. I want you to look at these questions as a quick cardiogram to see if your heart is strong enough to even begin considering ministry as a "calling." But you must let them work, take them deadly serious, drill down deep…

1. If others stop following Jesus, friends, family, a spiritual hero falls, will you stop? And if the answer is no, why not?

2. Why are you following Jesus — what do you want from him? In John 1:38 two disciples start following Jesus and he turns to them and asks, "What do you want?" How would you answer that? Or you can ask it like this, "What do you expect Jesus to give you since you are following him?" (Your answer here will direct the rest of your life.)

3. What if all of your expectations are not met, and you are even asked to suffer, will you still go on?

These are the root questions that uncover the condition of your heart and it is here we must start if we are going to make ministry a lifetime endeavor. The foundation must be solid because if it isn't, the superstructure is bound to fall. That is why I believe Paul would often use one word when he ministered — see if you can find it from the following verses:

1 Corinthians 5:8

_____

_____

_____


2 Corinthians 1:12

_____

_____

_____

_____

_____

_____


The keyword here is S_____!

If you are not sincere, get out! Stop and go somewhere else! This may be one of the only careers that completely depends upon you "living & proclaiming" (1 Timothy 4:12-13) what you are convinced is the real truth. Yes, it is impossible to know the full and exhaustive truth, but we must also accept that there is knowledge that can actually be apprehended. We can know things. If we don't have any truth to actually proclaim we are bound to fall into the trap of postmodernism's horrific syndrome of only asking questions and never being sure you can know anything for sure.

Did you know it is easy to ask questions? Anyone can level accusations at the hypocrisy of the church, or remain puzzled at the mystery of God's hiddenness, but it takes courage in our day to give answers and stand up against the naysayers on those answers. Malachi 2:7 says, "The words of a priest's lips should preserve knowledge of God, and people should go to him for instruction, for the priest is the messenger of the Lord of Heaven's Armies."

Do you believe we as ministers of the gospel have answers? I hope we have some, or why even bother becoming a teacher? And God will not suffer another Simon the Sorcerer (Acts 8:9-21). What was his main problem?

Just for the sake of simplicity and foundation building, I want to offer you three theological concepts that you must be firm on and you must hold fast to them! If you do not, you will have nothing to offer the hungry and weary people who come to learn from you. I believe these concepts are essential because they strike dead center at the heart of your belief in God and loyalty to his Son Jesus Christ.

1. **The Atonement of Christ (his death, burial, and resurrection) is where we find our hope.**

2 Corinthians 5:21

_____

_____

_____

Romans 3:23-26

_____

_____

_____

Hebrews 9:15

_____
_____
_____

Which verse stands out to you the most and why?

_____
_____
_____
_____

**2. God is Sovereign (He has full rights to do whatever he wants).**

Isaiah 46:8-11

_____
_____
_____

Romans 11:33-36

_____
_____
_____

1 Peter 1:19-20

_____

_____

_____

What if God was not 100% in control of your life
and he had a firm grip on the world's affairs, how
would that change the way you view ministry?

_____

_____

_____

3. **Mercy is why I am allowed to live and Grace is
why I continue living.**

Titus 3:3-7

_____

_____

_____

1 Corinthians 15:10

_____

_____

_____

Hebrews 4:16

_____

_____

_____

If God chose not to forgive, would there be any reason to love him?

_____

_____

_____

A minister of the living God must sincerely believe those things. It is vital to the health of a church and a person's life. And I am convinced that if I don't, when I stand in the pulpit or sit next to a dying person in the hospital, I will have nothing really to declare. I will have no hope to offer. And over time, if I am only playing the role of a pastor without the heart of one, God will eventually allow me to be proven both a liar and a charlatan which will end up in my utter humiliation. Malachi 2:8-9 says, "But you have turned from the way and by your teaching have caused many to stumble; you have violated the covenant with Levi, says the Lord Almighty. So I have caused you to be despised and humiliated before all the people, because you have not followed my ways but have shown partiality in matters of the law."

Be warned, people can spot a lying minister a mile away!

## The Pollutants to the Heart

So, take heed before you say that you have been entrusted with the secret things of God for sure (1 Corinthians 4:1). The heart is so easily deceived (Jeremiah 17:9), especially when people want to follow you — popularity and glory are intoxicating. This is every human's handicap: We are susceptible to the lies we tell ourselves and are quick to believe the lies we are told by others as well. Jesus warns that "If someone comes in his own name you so quickly receive him. How can you believe, when you receive glory from one another and do not seek the glory that comes from the only God?" (John 5:44-45). So for the heart to be foundationally strong, we must avoid the major or most toxic pollutants to the heart. And I believe there are three that have the potential to pervert the truth, and as a result will warp and poison the heart of all pastors (2 Peter 3:15-16):

### 1. ARROGANCE

When you are leading a group of curious, kind and trusting people and they in turn hand you both an important title and a pulpit to do your job, there is tremendous potential for you to let it go to your head. By nature, we crave a position of superiority and glory. Jesus in Matthew 23 warns about "loving the place of honor, having the best seats, being called teacher by others." Arrogance and believing you deserve to be recognized lies dormant in every human heart and it is ready to spring to life at the first whiff of praise.

Listen to what Augustine said about pride and arrogance, "Haughtiness or pride imitates God's lofty remove — but God alone is far removed from sin. It is the arrogation on the creature's part of something that properly belongs to God alone." According to Psalm 115:1, what belongs to God alone? _____

Never forget, an arrogant heart wishes to steal it from him. Oh, what a miserable trap arrogance is, and how easy it is to fall into. Because the more we are sure of ourselves, the less we will listen to the people pointing out our faults. And since we are human, we all have faults. Just look at 1 John 1:8: "If we claim to be without sin, we deceive ourselves and the truth is not in us." *Arrogance lies to us with a venomous tongue...*

How can we ever be wrong when we believe we are always right? This is not the heart of Christ. Philippians 2:3 & 5, "Do nothing out of selfish ambition or vain conceit. Rather, in humility value others above yourselves...Who being in the very nature of God did not consider equality with God something to be

20

GRASPED!" Woah! Who then am I to grasp if Jesus never once did? My rule of thumb for conquering this sneaky creep called arrogance is Isaiah 66:2b:

**Walk Humbly** — if someone points out a fault, then listen! They may be right, and most likely are. And don't take offense, humility understands that we have been made from dust.

**Tremble at His Word** — if your decisions are derived from his principles found in the scriptures and you believe they are in line with his will, you will be able to hold up under pressure. Your decisions and choices will not be based on your position or person, but rather on God's principles. And when you have firm convictions "YOU can truly STAND" even when the critics shoot their arrows and hurl their slings. And be assured, they will fire away. (See Psalm 64:3-4)


## 2. GREED

Jesus says we can serve only one of two masters: God or Money (See Matthew 6:24). Why do you think he chose these as the only two masters to choose from? I think the answer is obvious, they are the only two options that people will look at to find their safety, security, and significance. If I have enough money, why do I need to trust God? If I have enough money, why pray? If I have enough money, I don't need to go to him for my "daily bread" because I can buy whatever I need on my own. If I have enough money, people will respect and honor me.

Money allows me to live my life successfully, independent from God. This same attitude is the wicked rotten root of Adam's original sin. He wanted to be independent from God.

According to Genesis 3:5, what was Satan's big lie?

_____

_____

_____

So the more money a person has, the more secure they feel in themselves, like God, they can procure for themselves what they need and want, and accordingly the less they need to live by faith.

But our job as ministers of the Gospel is to promote faith, as Hebrews 11:6 says, "Without faith it is impossible to please God." And often God will use our life to show our complete dependence upon Him. The truth is, becoming a pastor is not the most lucrative career choice a person can make out in the market. He will often ask us to be content with little, drive rusted-out used cars, and forfeit the dream of having a cabin in the mountains. But God will always provide.

What does Hebrews 13:5-6 say?

_____

_____

_____

So does that mean I should not expect to be paid? Should I live in a mud hut and eat yams and rice? No, God wants us to live a normal life, so yes, you should be paid fairly. But remember, you are not in ministry for pay. Don't take a job because of the pay, but don't let the congregation use you as cheap labor where you end up killing your family in the process.

Look what Paul says in 1 Corinthians 9:9-10 :

_____

_____

_____

There is a balance here.

**QUESTION:** "How do you practically walk this tightrope?" Some ideas. . .

- Live in the "Median Wage" for those you serve (salary, benefits and investments).

- Increase pay as any wage earner would (ie: include

years of experience, education level, and amount of responsibility).

- Find a wage that will free you up to serve, without taking advantage of people's generosity.

### 3. LUST

Let's face it, this is where the battle is raging right now! Everyone must be honest, or they have already lost — lust is lurking, ready to pounce and destroy your ministry in the process. Lust in the form of pornography and hidden pleasure is available at the touch of a screen:

INTERNET
MOVIES
MAGAZINES
SMARTPHONES
AND OF COURSE...
SUMMER!

It is all around us and we are CALLED to be MATURE on this issue. Maturity, I believe, means that I don't do things that will secretly feed my lust. I also must exercise enough self-control where I am not afraid of ministering to beautiful people because I might be tempted to sin. This is why some pastors will only talk to men, which is sad because we are meant to pastor the whole church. How do you do this without falling into sexual sin?

## 1. Realize the Penalty of Lust is a Steep Price to Pay

My wife, my kids, my congregation are intimately linked with my fidelity. Numbers 32:23 are clear that your sin will find you out.

- Do you want to ruin your children? LUST.
- Do you want to kill your wife? LUST.
- Do you want to destroy the church? LUST.

Why is lust so dangerous? Because sin is crouching at the door and lust is like a shackle that won't leave you. And you must know that Job is very clear on this in Job 31:1 & 23. What does this verse mean to you?

_____

_____

_____

_____

## 2. Realize How Powerful a Temptation Sex Is!

Just being honest here: More ministries and families have been destroyed through lust issues than anything else. This is Satan's weapon of choice to destroy a church. So when fighting, prepare yourself for this onslaught. It is a battle! Look at the words scripture uses when fighting sins of the flesh. . .

- 1 Corinthians 9:27 — Is Paul serious?

- 1 Peter 4:1 — What does arming yourself mean?

- Revelation 2:20-23 — What is the penalty of sexual immorality?

## 3. CONCLUSION: How is Your Heart?

Is there anyone who you feel you can be honest with about your temptations? Is there anyone who you feel is positionally beneath you that you can spend time with and actually try to learn from them (this helps fight arrogance)? How is your family budget? Are you a big spender or are you genuinely content with your life situation? Never, never, never forget, if you don't have a healthy heart, you will become a very dangerous and deceptive person!!!

# 2

# Feeding Your Mind

"For the lips of a priest ought to
preserve knowledge, and from his
mouth men should seek instruction."
*Malachi 2:7*

Oh, what a gift is a mind that is alive! God's creative genius is displayed in each neuron that fires hot in the cerebral cortex of man. I believe the wonder of wondering is the one area of your life that directly affects your ministry the most. If you choose to be content with the basic learning you have initially received from college or seminary, your ministry will stall. It is like a sailing ship stuck in the doldrums without wind or current sitting heavy on the silent waters of a vast ocean. But if you continue to learn and improve your thinking, your job will get more exciting and the people in your congregation will love you for it (even though they will never realize it).

So enjoy your mind! Feed it and have fun in it. It is the greatest computer on the face of the earth, it is the one instrument that most resembles our maker, it is a gift that no price-tag can be put on. Developing the mind for the minister is more important than almost any other work. The reasons are not so obvious, but after a few years in real ministry the importance of thinking will start to show:

1. Week after week of teaching, preaching, leading small groups, visiting schools, counseling and even working with your kids all depend upon what is stored up in your gray matter. Read the following verses just to see how important thinking is…

   • Luke 6:45
   • Matthew 13:52

2. Thinking is your primary job and instructing is your primary role. Pastors all need to take Malachi 2:7-9 very seriously. What are the three principles you can take from these verses?

   1) _____
   2) _____
   3) _____

How does 2 Peter 3:16 correlate to the Malachi passage? How have you seen people misuse the Scriptures to their own demise?

_____

_____

_____


3. As a "protector of the sheep" you must be prepared to be ready to fight the issues of the mind as dark days approach. Look at these verses:


1 Timothy 4:1-2

_____

_____

_____


2 Timothy 2:25-26

_____

_____

_____


Acts 18:24-28

_____

_____

_____

On this issue of protecting, listen to this great quote by John Stott:

"Some will say the submission of our minds to the mind of Christ is an intellectual imprisonment. But no more so than the submission of our wills to the will of Christ is moral bondage. Certainly it ("taking every thought captive" – 2 Corinthians 10:5) is a surrender of liberty (ie. Intellectual Freedom), for no Christian can be a "free thinker". Yet it is that kind of surrender which is TRUE FREEDOM – freedom from our own miserable subjectivity, and freedom from bondage to the current whims and fancies of the world. Is it stunting to spiritual growth? No, it is ESSENTIAL to it, for Christian growth is nothing if it is not growth into Christ as Lord and head." (In other words, just as a true Christian is to guard their actions from ungodly behavior, so too must we guard our mind from ungodly philosophies)."

How have you seen "free thinking" adversely affect the gospel in a person's life?

_____

_____

_____

_____

_____

What do you think miserable subjectivity means?

_____

_____

_____

Look at how these verses back him up:

Colossians 2:8

_____

_____

_____

Romans 1:18-19, 21

_____

_____

_____

2 Corinthians 10:3-5

_____

_____

_____

I believe one of the biggest battles you are going to have in the realm of the mind is the "battle for the brilliant" — falling into the deadly trap of Intellectual Arrogance! Here is a quote about modern-day intellectual arrogance by a man I highly respect...

"Many Christian college students have allowed progressive understanding and critical study of art, music, philosophy and other areas of higher learning to cause arrogance and sophistication to plant a bitter root of doubt and disdain for their early Christian learning in their heart. Intellectual arrogance says that the rest of the world is clueless and ignorant. It believes that no one I know understands quite like me and the influential new teachers and friends that I now have here at college. This is simply not true, and in fact the hubris of high intellect is one of Satan's most deadly tools to throw impressionable Christians into vast mazes of confusion and destruction for many years of their young adult lives."

Please think hard on that. Since you are reading this book you understand the importance of the mind and you probably have the drive to improve and prepare yours for action. So I have a few suggestions on how to improve your thinking skills...

## A Thinking Plan

1. READ, READ, READ & READ AGAIN!

I have personally set up a reading schedule that I am

always following. I try to finish a good book every other week. I don't follow this religiously, but it is my continual guideline:

- Classics - Fiction and Non-fiction: this looks at the great writers and great books. Good literature opens your mind to the art of great communication and persuasion. (Suggested reads: Lord of the Rings Trilogy, "1984" G. Orwell)

- Current Theology and Christian Issues: these keep you aware of the trends in the church, and the new directions of the blowing of the Christian breeze. (Suggested reads: "Fools Talk" by O. Guinness, "Bad Religion" R. Douthat)

- Classic Theology & Biography: this allows the men of the past to speak into your life and usually they are smarter than writers of today because they had much more time to think. (Suggested reads: "On Being a Theologian of the Cross" Gerard Forde, "Prayer" O. Halleseby, "Bonhoeffer" Eric Metaxas)

## 2. UNDERSTAND THE ANTAGONISTS AND THINKING OF THE ENEMIES OF CHRIST

Read the Christian haters, it makes you think and learn

how to defend your faith. It will also force you to know the Scriptures on your own to find how God answers the same questions. Learn the popular arguments of the day and be ready for how the enemy thinks. Suggested reads: "Rage Against God" Peter Hitchens, "The God Delusion" Richard Dawkins.

## 3. STUDY THE HISTORY OF PHILOSOPHY AND DIFFERENT RELIGIONS

Read Francis Schaeffer for philosophic overviews and then pick your interest (Kierkegaard, Luther, Edwards).

## 4. WRITE A BLOG, WORK ON A BOOK

This will help you test out your ideas, see if anyone is interested or stirred by what you have to say, and then go public with it. Not only will people be brutally honest with you, but it will force you to write better knowing you will be read! There is nothing more humbling than honest feedback.

## 5. CHOOSE A MENTOR

This is probably the most important way to become a good thinker. Find a writer who speaks to your heart, and read all you can that they wrote. This is like finding a good friend you allow to speak into your life. Not every writer will speak to you. But the one that does will really stir your mind to love to think. So find one and then make them your guide (Piper, Luther, Schaeffer, Lewis).

## 6. LEARN HOW TO SPOT LOGICAL FALLACIES

There are abundant resources out there on what a logical fallacy is. Everywhere you go people are using statements that do not follow logical trains of thought. Whether it be "straw man" arguments, "non-sequiturs" or "slippery slope" deductions. The more your thinking patterns follow clear thinking and logic the more precise and potent your teaching will be. Too many pastors in the pulpit have never learned logic so they come to conclusions that cannot be supported by reason or revelation.

We live in the age of image. Sight and feeling have overtaken hearing and thinking. And as a result, if I make something appear to be true, even if it isn't logical, people are quick to believe nonsense. As one famous writer once said, "Let my people THINK!" The world is desperate to hear real answers from some mature minds.

# 3

# Navigating Your Family

"Now the overseer must...manage his
own family well and see that his
children obey him with proper respect."
*1 Timothy 3:4*

It was a sleepy day. In my boredom there I sat on
the couch randomly flipping through the television
channels when I stopped at the Christian station. The
man speaking happened to be a pastor in the Bahamas
and he said something that struck me as profound:

"Too many times pastors view the church as their
wife, and so they end up spending all their time with
the church. But this isn't true, the church is the bride of
Christ, and in truth, these pastors are committing
adultery with Christ's bride! Go home and spend time
with your wife."

Wow, what a statement, the church isn't the pastor's bride, it is Jesus' bride. As one pastor said, "Men too often neglect their family just so they can have a sexy ministry." What do you think a sexy ministry means?

_____

_____

_____

When people say they want to do "great things" for God, do you think it ever includes taking care of your family first? This is such an important area of life for the pastor to navigate, and you must really think through your first obligation, "For better or for worse, for richer or for poorer..." because I believe a pastor's natural tendency is to feel total responsibility for the progress of the church above every other concern. Pastoring is a heavy responsibility because it feels like everything falls on their shoulders. But don't take the bait because the church is Jesus' bride, and he knows how to care for it without you, as the pastor, losing your family in the process.

### EASIER SAID THAN DONE!

Enormous pressure is being put on ministers these days, and if not watched closely, these pressures can kill a family. Here is a satirical resume' churches look for in a pastor:

# The Perfect Pastor

* He condemns sin roundly but never hurts anyone's feelings. He works from 8 AM until midnight and is also the church janitor. He makes $40 a week, wears good clothes, drives a good car, buys good books, and donates $30 a week to the church. He is 29 years old and has 40 years' experience.

* He never forgets a name and spends most of his time praying to God. He also knows when somebody is sick and needs visitation even without anyone telling him about it.

* He remembers everyone's birthdate and of course, their anniversary dates as well. Before and after services, he never fails to speak to each person present and will also take the time to listen to you for 15 minutes and pray for each person no less than 10 minutes after listening to them.

* The perfect pastor always smiles and tells you what you want to hear. He also goes out to eat after church with each individual family, spreading his time evenly between all, and he also pays for all their meals.

* He makes 15 home visits a day and is always in his office to be handy when needed, and always has time for church council and all of its committees. He never misses the meeting of any church organization and is always busy evangelizing the unchurched.

* The perfect pastor preaches exactly 10 minutes.

## The Real Pressures

**Obvious Ones:**

* Achievement Expectations: Preach well, counsel well, keep new people coming to the church while always making the budget.

* Apostolic Expectations: Be godly, be wise, be confrontative, be right, and be blameless.

**Not-so-Obvious Ones:**

* Appearance Expectations: Be happy, be funny, be good looking, and be caring and kind.

* Availability Expectations: Be there when I call, be

there each weekend to preach, be my friend.

Which expectations are more demanding for the Pastor?

_____

_____

_____

Which expectations are more demanding for the Pastor's wife?

_____

_____

_____

And can a couple in ministry fulfill all these expectations?

_____

_____

_____

The truth is, if you try to constantly meet these expectations, the amount of stress that you will be living under will be too much for anyone to bear. It will eventually destroy you and your family. That is why burnout, depression and isolation are common ailments ministers feel after many years of serving the local church.

So what must first be understood above all else is that you can't do it! You will never be all things to all people. So you must decide what your family can reasonably handle before you join any given church, and then be ready to take flack for the expectations you can't meet. And here is the hard part, you must do all that without growing bitter. Bitterness is like poison in your soul, it will cause you to feel like Elijah after he took on the priests of Baal alone.

Look at 1 Kings 19:13-18, what was Elijah's complaint?

_____

_____

_____

When you find yourself offering to God the same type of complaints, be careful, a bitter root may be growing. So face it now, meeting and satisfying everyone's expectation is "Impossible!"

WHY IMPOSSIBLE? (I thought with Jesus nothing is impossible?)

June 12, 2006 — "Mary Winkler, half of what has been described as 'a perfect couple,' was indicted by a grand jury today on first-degree murder charges in the

March 22 shooting of her husband, the minister Matthew Winkler.

He was the passionate young minister and she, his quiet, substitute-teacher wife, beloved and respected in the town of Selmer, Tenn. The alleged murder has left his congregants desperate to find a motive to explain why, seemingly out of nowhere, Mary Carol Winkler allegedly shot her husband dead and ran away with their three daughters."

The question of the above case is why? When you read the story closely, the expectations that are placed on the wife, husband and kids to be perfect can emotionally kill you, and if you give in to them you are placing impossible burdens on your family. You cannot do that as a pastor. So the bigger issue is, "How do you avoid that?" Learn the three "L's":

1. Consider what you can LOSE.
2. LISTEN to your family's perspective.
3. LEAD them through the garbage with grace.

## Lose

Ask yourself this: What would it be like if you lost your wife and kids because of your ambition? Is their destruction worth being famous and successful?

One of the most spiritual books I ever read was,

"The Shofar Blew" written by Francine Rivers. If you are considering ministry, I say this is a must read. It is a book that puts into perspective what is really important. Fame, big numbers, sermons that "wow", and happy congregants mean nothing as compared to having the love of a wife and the respect of your kids. If you can drill that into your mind, you will avoid the snare of "I must do great things for God". Here are two questions to help with proper assessment:

When you die, what do you want your wife to say about you?

_____

_____

_____

When you die, what do you want your kids to say about you?

_____

_____

_____

Your answers to those two questions could be the most important directives for your whole life. I believe the problem with most marriages is that success is placed before relationship. But success to me is how those closest to me view me; and if my sons and daughters love their dad, I won! Who cares if I preach like Spurgeon and perform like Graham – my family is my priority. Jesus will use me if I am faithful, and he will always accomplish what he set out to do. Never forget 1 Thessalonians 5:24

## Listen

If you agree with the above conclusion then naturally you must monitor the perspectives of your family and listen. Listen to your wife, she is your helpmeet, so let her help. Look at this verse:

1 Peter 3:7 – What does considerate mean? What if you don't listen according to that verse?

How about your kids, do they see you, do they hear from you, and do you let them in? 4 ideas to include kids:

- Let them always be able to interrupt you about important matters.

- Let them be your teachers in their field of expertise: music, video games, school, and their world of ideas.

- Don't pressure them to live up to the external codes

of the people in your congregation.

- Make their events your priority: Band, Sports, Theatre, and even Track. Sitting at a stadium all afternoon to watch one event may be long, but it does show love!

We are here to be real people who live real lives; not Saviors of the world. Be there for your family, for that is what matters most.

## Lead

One warning must be issued that is extremely important: Your family is not always right! There will be times when your family will have opinions on the lives of people in your church or issues of church polity where they are not fully informed or wise, and it behooves you as the leader of the flock not to let their subjectivity affect your objectivity.

For instance:

1. Don't share confidential information with your wife or kids that they shouldn't be allowed to hear. People will tell you things that must be for your ears alone. You will be tempted to go home and share each

nugget with your wife, but wisdom says "Be Careful." I have personal guidelines for sharing with my wife:

- Don't share if it will affect her opinion negatively about a church member.

- Don't share if a person said something to hurt you and it will cause her to angrily defend you.

- Don't share details of board meetings that don't involve her, but would rile her up if she heard them. And don't allow her frustration to cause you to influence a board and their decision.

- Don't bad mouth your wife in front of leadership.

2. As a father, one of your main goals is to shield your children from the ill-will that exists in the normal life of church relationships. I believe "PK" (pastor's kids) bitterness occurs because pastors unwisely inform their kids about the problems of people at church when they do not have the discerning capacity to handle it. So protect them by speaking highly of people in the home, or not revealing names of people that they know who may have disagreed or argued with you.

3. And NEVER, EVER, treat your kids as better than other kids because they are the pastor's kids. Learn to treat them equally, and have similar expectations as you would other kids in the church. Your child is a child, so let them grow up in innocence and not under the weight of ministerial expectations.

## Something Fun

The best way to end this section on family is simply by striving to make your home one that is a joy. Let your kids be your hobby. Let your wife be your friend. Keep home life happy. And when you do, you will find a welcome refuge from the onslaughts of ministry.

**Some closing thoughts on family:**

- I believe Jesus laughs, a lot. Your kids need to see that.

- I believe your wife has enough just raising kids, therefore only expect out of her what you would a regular follower of Jesus Christ in the church.

- I believe Satan wants to attack you and he does it by going after that which is precious to you. Protect your kids in prayer.

- If your life doesn't match your sermon, your kids are the first to know.

- Discipleship is best seen in father and child relationships; if your child doesn't want Jesus, who then in your congregation will?

- Have fun, no one else does!

# 4

# Maintaining a Devotional Life

"One thing I ask of the Lord, this is what I seek: that I may dwell in the house of the Lord all the days of my life."
*Psalm 27:4*

**GUILT!** Here it is, the subject that can cause you to mercilessly wallow in self-pity:

PRAYER
DEVOTIONS
BIBLE READING
TIME WITH GOD

How do I go about talking about this without hypocrisy and false piety? How do I talk about this without unloading enormous guilt on the listener? I have decided to just be honest.

**CONFESSION:** This is the biggest struggle of my life because I have never lived up to my expectations in this area. The reasoning goes like this:

* If God is the greatest being and the most powerful being, then prayer is the greatest thing I could ever do.

* But if I were honest, which is tough to do, I don't see him, I can't touch him, I am not sure he really is answering, and I am not that stimulated when I pray.

* So, I often feel like I must do work that looks like I am working. Because hard work accomplishes tasks and praying is just sending words to the air...

**OR IS IT?** Both Jesus and Paul see prayer as a gift given to the child of God to meet with his Father. Over and over again in scripture Jesus went to pray to get away from the crush of the crowd. Paul said that he devoted himself to prayer and even wrestled in prayer for those he loved.

So ask yourself honestly, how is your prayer life?

_____

_____

_____

Do you feel like you spend adequate time with God?

_____

_____

_____

Are you and God intimate?

_____

_____

_____

When pastors are honest about this, the overall feeling in their heart is failure. And failure causes you to want to run from God instead of running to him. So how do we change this if prayer is intended to be our most powerful tool in ministry?

## Mindsets That Can Change Your Walk:

To destroy guilt and drive a proper motivation for meeting with God, I believe there are a couple of essential attitudes we must adopt as we approach the prayer closet:

**1) FREEDOM:** We are not condemned because we fail to meet with God! Do you believe that?

Romans 8:1

_____

_____

_____

Romans 8:34

_____

_____

_____

1 John 1:7-9

_____

_____

_____

Which verse speaks the most to you on the subject of freedom?

_____

_____

_____

**2) BLESSING:** We actually can choose how much grace we want to receive. Do you want the blessing of God in your life? If yes — Pray. Do you want to know him more? If yes — Read His Word. Do you want to find a joy that is not contrived or dependent on circumstances? If yes — Fight for Intimacy with God!

Imagine if God said that there was a table loaded with the finest of food and drink in the other room. All you had to do was open the door. You don't deserve the food, it is a gift from God to give you strength and joy. But to get to the food all you have to do is open the door. That is it. And that is prayer.

Sounds simple, doesn't it? This is known as conditional grace. God has given his children loads and loads of tremendous promises, all we have to do is follow his instructions to get to the promises. This is the essence of faith: I believe that God rewards those who earnestly seek him. And prayer is the most direct and pure way to obtain his favor. It is not a burden, but rather it is a blessing. Do you believe this?

**3) ACQUIRED DELIGHT:** Do you like coffee? Did you always like coffee? How does a person learn to like coffee? You must keep drinking it — and a lot of it! Growing in conditional grace is acquired the same way, through habit. But the goal is delight, not perfection, acquisition or position — delight. Many people come to God to get things or to be better disciples than others, but we must learn to come to God for him and him alone:

Psalm 42:1

_____

_____

_____

Psalm 63:1-2

_____

_____

_____

Psalm 73:25-26

_____

_____

_____

Are these Psalms true of your life?

_____

_____

_____

Which of these statements seem foreign to you?

_____

_____

_____

# HOW DO YOU APPROACH THESE HABITS?

"Relationship" is not a formula, it just is. Simply put, you must learn to nurture your delight in God in your own way. Sure there are helps and ideas and guidelines, but my walk with God is unique because the walk with my brother Jesus and my Father God is unique. Look to your own family — does everyone relate the same with your dad? Do you talk the same way to your brother as your sister talks to him? No, that is because everyone's relationship is different. So it is with the person of God. Because God is a person.

## MY PERSONAL EXPERIENCE

- Journaling: I have found that writing down prayers and wrestling through scripture on paper focuses me in ways that mere talking never does. It forces me to focus my thoughts and sharpen my language. I find much of modern prayer is loaded with clichés and rarely do you write out clichés when you are forced to put down thoughts.

- Walking: When I go to the woods and walk with Jesus I seem to really open up. Oftentimes I yell out my frustrations, I sing songs of praise, I read the Psalms out loud in a British accent, I argue and even ponder single thoughts or verses. I think the disciples during Jesus' day loved to talk with him while they walked. As my own father once told me, "Walking takes the wrinkles out of your mind."

- Memorization: I find that a verse of power, when memorized, changes me and my outlook. When you chew on truth it gets into you. That is what meditation does (i.e. Galatians 2:20 has changed my life).

- Fasting: This is serious business with God. If I need to pray about an issue of serious concern I fast. I forfeit food and drink for a day (you still need water), and when I have hunger pangs, I turn to God in prayer. Just as I need food to physically survive, fasting shows how I need God to spiritually survive.

- Reading: Good writers are like good friends – they challenge you in ways that you can't arrive at on your own. I also heard that reading great authors is like getting wisdom from some of the smartest men and women who ever lived. You can have a discussion with them in your very own living room. Read, read, and read!

To me, devotional life must be a delight, not a chore, not a work, not an accomplishment. It is finding an avenue that helps you fall in love with the God who is there.

Look back on your walk with God, what are the tools that have helped you feel closest to him? Why not try to start again?

## GENERAL IDEAS:

- Devotional Studies: These are designed studies by Christian authors who force you to grapple with a text. To begin, a great devotional that is still sold today at most Christian bookstores is "Experiencing God." Also, try reading "With" by Skye Jethani — this is an amazing devotional book.

- Prayer Partner: Is there someone, or a group of people that can meet with you regularly to pray? Our church started a monthly prayer meeting on Tuesday nights called "The Gathering." It is so refreshing, I still can't understand why people don't come. It makes me sad.

- Memory Program: The Navigators have a wonderful scripture memory program that regularly forces you to digest scripture. Try it out!

- Retreats: Go to a place for a few days to just get away and meet with God. Try being silent for a whole day. It might just change your life!

## The Mountain & The Lodge

Many of you who are considering full-time ministry have been faithful church attendees as well. You have been going to church for years and Sunday church attendance has been a very important part of your life. Because of that fact, many of you have been involved in a number of ministries, classes, outreaches, and church programs throughout the years. You have seen great things happen in your life and the lives of others.

You see, whether you know it or not you most likely are in the lodge stage of your Christian life. I am not talking about your age, I am talking about your position in life. Let me explain…

Imagine you are going hiking in the majestic Rocky Mountains around Denver, CO. On your trip you bring a back-pack, climbing/camping gear, hiking stick, and trail mix that will last you for months. After the first couple of weeks, you have traversed the foothills, made some daring climbs up steep mountain faces, fought off an angry black bear, viewed some wonderful morning vistas, and even crossed some huge chasms in the rock by a steel cable. Wow, what an adventure! At points, you didn't think you could make it, but through skill and perseverance you steadily make it up and down the magnificent range.

Then one day, after climbing a very severe cliff of rock you reach the top of a mountain bluff. Straight ahead is a quaint log cabin. The sign says, "Welcome, all weary travelers. Make yourself at home." As you take off the heavy gear and turn on the lights you are amazed by the general warmth of the place: Cozy couches, stocked cupboard and fridge, soft downy bed, and a roaring fireplace. You notice on the mantle there are trophies and plaques commemorating your hard work at the climb. As you sit there you notice a door that is barely open with a cold draft of icy air pouring through. You go to close it and as you look out the back the giant mountain is waiting for you!

Most of us don't want to get up off the couch and head back out into the cold. We like to look at our trophies, consider ourselves to have arrived, pat ourselves on the back and say, "Well done, good and faithful servant." But wait — isn't that God's property? Don't steal it from him.

The truth is, Christianity is never meant to be a place we arrive, it is a journey to continue. Having a strong devotional life makes walking with Jesus as exciting as climbing a mountain: New views, wonderful trails, and exhilaration at each new turn. Don't forfeit joy by sitting on a couch. Don't ever be satisfied!

# 5

# Shepherding Sheep

"Here is a trustworthy saying, if anyone
sets his heart on being an overseer, he
desires a noble task."
*1 Timothy 3:1*

For the people of Jesus' day, shepherding sheep was a normal, yet mundane occupation; I guarantee you it wasn't looked at as a particularly praiseworthy job. In fact, being a shepherd was lonely, hazardous, and always humble. A man standing alone, in the rain, late at night under the twinkling stars of a quiet sky, or trying to run from the rays of a hot uncaring sun. A shepherd must stay vigilant out in the open fields night and day, be ready for a sheep to wander away at any moment, and keep an eye out for predators licking their chops wanting to devour one of his juicy little lambs.

Sheep were always prone to danger, which for the experienced shepherd is not surprising. Why not? Because the animal has a pea for a brain! Consider this actual news story:

"Hundreds of sheep followed their leader off a cliff in eastern Turkey, plunging to their deaths this week while shepherds looked on in dismay. Four hundred sheep fell 16 feet to their deaths in a ravine in Van province near Iran but broke the fall of another 1,100 animals who survived. Shepherds from a nearby village neglected the flock while eating breakfast, leaving the sheep to roam free. The loss to local farmers was estimated at $74,000." As one writer commented, "One sheep wandered off a cliff and 1,499 others just followed along. Can you picture it? 1,500 sheep, each walking off a cliff, one after the other. Soon they were piled so deep that the ones at the bottom were crushed to death and the ones on top were lying on a big downy -soft pillow. It is completely absurd and tells us one important fact about sheep and the first reason sheep absolutely need a shepherd: they are not the smartest animals in the world. In fact, they may well be just about the dumbest animals in the world."

Isaiah 53:6 uses this same picture of a sheep to describe all of us in our sinful condition, "All we like sheep have gone astray; we have turned — every one —

to his own way." If you are called to be a pastor/ shepherd of a church, you will be asked to work with wandering sheep every day. Sounds like a great career move, doesn't it? Chasing sheep! Well, that is exactly what God calls the pastor to do. Jesus even asked Peter in John 21:17, "Peter do you love me? Feed my sheep." Does this sound like a noble task to you? Well God says it is in I Timothy 3:1.

How would you define a noble task, and how should I view a noble task?

_____

_____

_____

Do you believe pastoring (taking care of sheep) is a noble task? If yes, why?

_____

_____

_____

People don't realize it, but not just anybody can do this job. A person can't just walk off the street and decide they want to be a pastor; it is granted to the few who God has gifted and called. I find it is rare to find a person who likes to watch sheep. Seldom is the person who will give up their life, their freedom, their desire for personal independence to spend their life caring for simple sheep. I can't tell you how many times I have heard, "Why do you choose to meet with people that don't really give much back to you or appreciate the sacrifice?" All I can say is that God has put the desire in me to do it.

In some sense, watching sheep doesn't require you to be a brilliant mathematician, a creative writer, or even a high caliber leader. But it does ask you to be made of rock-solid stuff, the kind of stuff that demands you to be the type of person who. . .

* WON'T COMPLAIN

* WORKS HARD

* HANGS IN THERE — EVEN WHEN EVERYONE ELSE BAILS

Out of these three, which do you think is the hardest and why?

_____

_____

_____

A noble job is noble for the sheer fact it will prove

to be both dangerous and strategic. Listen to what Eugene Peterson says about it:

"Why do pastors have such a hard time being pastors? Because we are awash in idolatry. Where two or three are gathered together and God comes up, a committee is formed for making an idol. We want gods that are not gods so we can be 'as gods'. The idolatry to which pastors are conspicuously liable is not personal, but vocational, the idolatry of religious career that we can take charge and manage."

I especially think the reason pastoring is so hard these days is because there is overwhelming contempt in our culture for any kind of authority. People don't like to be told what to do, especially by a pastor. Look at a new home church's beliefs about church that was on their website:

"Jesus is the head of the church, not the 'pastor.' Unfortunately, pastors have become the functional head ('boss') of the church for most people. That is unhealthy and dangerous. . . Church isn't somewhere you go, it's something you are. It's something you do. So, yes, we believe many churches have made a practice of wasting way too much money on elaborate buildings and large staff salaries. More of our money should be used to 'church' ourselves in the world, where we work to repair, restore, renew, re-create, and reconcile.

The clergy/laity/(pastor/congregation) divide is debilitating to the Body. From the beginning, God's design was that mankind (men & women) would collectively represent Him. Even the ancient prophets dreamed of the day that everyone would be as a priest. Power and authority in the Church is not positional, but revolving and shared. We are to submit to one another, side by side, not over and under. The authority given to us by Christ is to serve. Therefore, our elders must be the greatest servants among us!"

What do you agree with about this statement?

_____

_____

_____

What do you disagree with about this statement?

_____

_____

_____

How can the following verses help crystalize the concept of pastor in your mind:

Hebrews 13:7, 17

_____

_____

_____

1 Peter 5:1-4

_____

_____

_____

Ephesians 4:11-13

_____

_____

_____

Why do you think there is such contempt for authority in our society?

_____

_____

_____

What happens when there is a sharp dispute in the church where two groups of people see an issue two different ways and they cannot agree — who wins?

_____

_____

_____

How did the church handle it in Acts 6:1-7?

_____

_____

_____

I want to end this section by looking at an email that I sent to a ministry friend who was really struggling in his ministry and wanted to quit because he didn't think what he was doing was that important. He was frustrated that people really didn't seem to either listen or change under his leadership. They seemed to wander and quit following just like sheep. He started questioning both himself and even the role of a pastor, is it even needed? So instead of teaching him, and telling him it is important, I took the Socratic method of asking him questions. Here they are. . .

If you could somehow see the invisible reality behind your ministry, what would it look like?

_____

_____

_____

Do you really think there are demons and angels vying for the souls in your congregation?

_____

_____

Who are you competing against? The world, the flesh and the Devil or other pastors and their programs to see who is the best in God's eyes?

_____

_____

_____

For me, I answer my call to pastoring and perseverance daily by believing that each word I utter in "sincerity" has behind it the power of life and death. If I utter words to make people happy it ends most of the time in catering to pride, and pride always leads to death. If I utter convictions and exhortations and encouragement based on scriptural fact, I believe life through the Spirit will be produced. With that being said, march on, stay vigilant, and protect the sheep... just like Jeremiah in Jeremiah 15:19.

Memorize it, it will save your ministry!

# 6

# Mastering Speech

"We proclaim him, admonishing and teaching
everyone perfect in Christ. To this end I
labor, struggling with all his energy which so
powerfully works in me."
*Colossians 1:28-29*

There is a new and persuasive argument on ministry philosophy these days and it goes like this:

"Growing up, how many sermons do you really remember? Probably very few. But how many people and their relationships that influenced you do you remember? Probably a lot. So what do you think is more important, preaching or relationships?"

This is what you would call not just a leading question, but a bad case of logic. First of all, this question is setting you up to agree that relationships are the most important thing. Who is going to argue with that? But secondly, it is pitting relationships against preaching, as if you have to choose one or the other. But with Christ everything is important!

The biggest problem with this question is that it fails to address just how important preaching, public speaking and the tool that speech is to your ministry. A pastor is a herald, a spokesman for Christ the King, so it really is everything. Just look at a couple of verses and explain how important preaching really is to God:

Jeremiah 1:9-10

_____

_____

_____

Malachi 2:7-9

_____

_____

_____

Acts 2:37

_____

_____

_____

Col 1:28-29

_____

_____

_____

Some people called to ministry are not as drawn to preaching as others, but it still is the life blood of the church. Never forget, God spoke and the world came to be. So too, preaching is the continuation of his life giving power.

## Preaching is Incarnational

What is the incarnation? (see John 1:1 & 17)

_____

_____

_____

"IN the beginning was the Word and the Word was with God and the Word was God. . . The Word became flesh and dwelt among us." Preaching is the "Word of God" coming through the preacher's flesh: his life, his attitudes, his actions. How does this happen?

1) **FIRST STEP:** Know the Word so well that it speaks and not you!

Do you know the difference between "eisegesis" and "exegesis?" It is crucial to preaching: eisegesis is when your opinion is arrogantly placed high above God's perfect words, and exegesis is when scripture is given complete reign above your meager tottering opinion. The power in preaching comes through the truth that God wants communicated (exegesis), not through the opinions you want to espouse (eisegesis). Truth, in this case, is **"That which corresponds to the way things really are."** Only the word of God is true truth, it properly explains, without exaggeration or pretension, life as it exists both on heaven and earth.

Opinions of human beings are often slanted, ignorant, blind, selfish, and impure. God's truth is just the opposite. James 3:13-18 is very clear on this.

Put it into your own words:

_____

_____

_____

_____

_____

_____

So before a man preaches, the text must rule over his mind rather than him ruling over the text. A true herald of God promises to "tell the truth, the whole truth, and nothing but the truth". There are three very important ingredients to help you do this:

**1. Integrity:** Hermeneutical research must be done, and done well. Make sure you are not stretching words to fit your agenda. Look at what God says in 2 Peter 3:16-17. What is the warning that Peter gives?

_____

_____

_____

**2. Sincerity:** Only preach what you personally believe to be true; not what you are supposed to say or you were trained to say in college and seminary. Say what God's word says.

**3. Humility:** If you are trying to impress or you are not fully sold on your conclusions, don't preach it. First live it before you proclaim something that you can't personally live out.

2) **SECOND STEP:** Know your own heart so it makes the Word real!

You are living in a real-world, you have real fears, questions and concerns — allow the text to address them. Make sure each sermon answers many of these questions:

1. What bothers me about the text, be honest and tell the congregation?

2. What excites me about the text?

3. What cultural myth is this destroying?

4. What cultural sin is it confronting?

5. How does this change my perspective of God?

People need to hear how you view these things, if they don't, the text will hang limp, and they will not experience incarnational truth. A good preacher is first and foremost a wrestler. He wrestles with God about his own heart.

3) **THIRD STEP:** Plead with God to anoint your words!

D. L. Moody said there were times in his ministry when the Spirit of God took over his words. That is what I am talking about, as Zechariah 4:6 says, "This is the word of the LORD to Zerubbabel: Not by might, nor by power, but by my Spirit, says the LORD of hosts." There will be times when you are speaking, but

God's power will cut people to the heart (Acts 2:37). And then you know you are watching God work. How does it happen? Pray his Promises: God responds to his promises. Here are some of the promises that God gives.

- Boldness: Ephesians 6:19

- Clarity: Colossians 4:2-4

- Conviction: Acts 2:37

- Understanding: Philippians 1:9-11

- Love for God: Ephesians 3:16-21

Charles Spurgeon said, "The only thing that gives me courage to preach week after week is that I say to myself before I preach, 'I believe in the Holy Spirit, I believe in the Holy Spirit, I believe in the Holy Spirit.'"

## Dead Men

Dr. Erwin Lutzer would bring his preaching class to a graveyard and he would tell them to stand over the grave and start preaching. The students were encouraged to use their best illustrations and best logic in argument. And then he said, "Preach, as loud and as strong as you can." So for the next fifteen minutes, the students preached until exhaustion. When the 15 minutes were over he said, "This is what you are doing every Sunday. Eloquence won't raise the dead, brilliance won't raise the dead, and argument won't raise the dead. Only the life-giving word, excited by the Spirit of God and communicated through a pure vessel will see blind eyes opened and deaf ear loosed." So never forget…

YOU ARE PREACHING TO THE DEAD & HIS WORD IS THE ONLY THING THAT HAS THE POWER TO RAISE THEM!

# 7

# I Need a Rest!

"Now we who have believed enter that
rest, just as God has said."
*Hebrews 4:3*

What does the word Sabbath mean to you?

_____

_____

_____

Did God really get tired when he made the world?

_____

_____

_____

God used his rest as an example for us to stop
because we really are not as important as we think we
are to the workings of the world. Sometimes, as a

pastor, I think we forget this. If we could be honest, this is what we really believe:

- The ministry would die if I quit working.
- People would be lost without my leadership.
- If I let go of control people will mess it up.

Often pastors go into ministry because their Type A personalities drive them to get stuff done. We feel we must be busy for God or we are wasting our time on earth. Be very careful when these thoughts start creeping in because they could eventually start to emotionally deplete life from your soul and ruin your ministry. Never forget this. . .

1 Corinthians 10:12

_____

_____

_____

This truth will save your skin. And the best way to guard against thinking too highly of yourself is taking rest or enjoying Sabbath.

## What Sabbath Is Not

Sunday: For the pastor, Sunday tends to be the day that he works the hardest. Sunday is not the replacement of Saturday on the Jewish calendar. Nor is the idea of taking a Sabbath the day in which you are quiet and sleep and make sure nobody does anything. So often the concept of Sabbath is seen as a day of complete boredom and seriousness. That Sabbath is a day God wants me to be miserable. How do you feel about the word Sabbath?

---

---

---

---

## What Sabbath Is

Well then, what is the Sabbath, especially for the pastor?

**1) State of MIND:** It is allowing your reputation and success to rest solely on the work of God. If you really believe you are his child, and there is no condemnation being identified with Christ, then start resting. Romans 8:31 screams that God is in your corner fighting for you, so you can stop working and let him fight. In Christ, you are loved! Think about this a minute. Our striving usually comes from trying to meet some unspoken series of expectations, cross off some list of demands, or prove your loyalty to an angry magistrate (Matthew 25:24). But if God is satisfied with you, then rest in him. If you are not sure if God is satisfied, meditate on what God said about Jesus in Luke 3:22, because when you are in him he is saying it about you too!

Never forget this verse — Galatians 1:10 — it may save your ministry. What does it mean to you?

_____

_____

_____

So if you are pleasing to God, then rest!

**2) A DAY to set aside:** I believe the original intent of Sabbath was designed so people would be forced to stop — stop everything from working to worrying. It was a planned time to trust God instead of self. It was a teaching tool of faith that God will do what he promised. And the principle still remains: Out of a non -legalistic perspective, stopping one day is a gift. The human body needs to stop, and if you don't plan it, you will not do it.

One day of the week is crucial to stop your work and let resting in God be your pursuit. As a pastor, what day is good for you? Some people advise not to take Monday because you are not at your best, but for me, it is the day I need to stop the world and enjoy

God. Let him slow me down, and not feel guilty for it.

**3) A SEASON of refreshment:** This is not a vacation, this is a period of time where you get away and focus on God. It could be a one month Sabbatical or a designated time to pray, think and stop. You need to try to find a good chunk of time each year when you can free your mind up to be with God. Very few pastors do this, which is why very few hear from God.

## What Do You Do on the Sabbath?

My simple answer is this: ENJOY GOD!

Sabbath is intended to be a blessing, not drudgery. And you need to do those things that bring you to points of:

* Gratitude: Gratefulness to be alive and you must find those things that allow you to do this.

* Refreshment: What allows you to rest and get the wrinkles out? This isn't selfish, it is necessary.

* Awe & Inspiration: Where can you go, what can you read, what can you do that brings you to wonder?

FIND IT, AND DO IT. RESULTS:

If you take Sabbath you will be a different person, a changed person, a person that walks with God.

Genesis 5:22

_____

_____

_____

It is not too hard, and its mere words won't convince you. So this is the chapter of being, not thinking. Are you ready to enjoy God? So Go!

# 8

# Urgent!!!

"Be swift to hear, slow to speak and
slow to grow angry."
*James 1:19*

The phone rings. . .

*"Pastor, I need to talk with you immediately, can I
come in?"*

*"Pastor, my wife just left the house with her suitcase
packed; can I come over?"*

*"Pastor, the ambulance took my husband to ER...
Help!!!"*

When these moments come in your ministry,
which they will, how will you respond?

1) Not pick up the phone?

2) Run immediately to help, leaving everything, to be the rescuer?

3) Offer some trite statement like, "Don't worry, God is still on the throne"?

## Three Responses

I propose three ways to handle situations like this:

**1) James 1:19**

---

---

---

Being a Savior isn't your prime job, it is being a path to the Savior and that takes wisdom. So to get wisdom you must first listen. As you listen, get a pad and paper and write down the obvious stuff. . .

A. Name, number and time of the call.
B. List the main points that they say, questions they have, and feelings they share.

After a while, God will start showing you the degree

of urgency of each situation because over time you will see that there are a lot of selfish people in the church, and selfish people make everything urgent. Sometimes they will call a pastor to get a mouse in the basement, or solve an argument over which movie to watch, or to get advice about a cut on their child's elbow. People want to be rescued, NOW!

When you are quick to respond to every moment of crisis, you may be forfeiting your important time with God and family for the selfish wants of others. It will surprise how Jesus responded to the demands of others. Read the following verses and formulate some "principles of response" from Jesus life. This may save you later in your busy ministry:

Luke 12:14, John 2:3-4, Luke 4:42-44

---

---

---

---

---

---

---

---

2)  **Proverbs 11:14**

_____

_____

_____

Get advisors, use your elders, invite your fellow pastors to help. Too many pastors are mavericks and when you enter into a hotbed situation you may be very vulnerable. Satan loves to isolate you and he makes you feel like you are the only one who cares.

PARABLE OF HOLDING ROPES:

Imagine you are walking down a wooded trail path alone. You are simply trying to enjoy the day, breathing in the fresh air and getting some much-needed sunshine. Half-way on your walk, you come to a clearing where your path leads you to a narrow wooden bridge that stretches across a steep rock-faced gulley below. The view from the bridge is breath-taking. As you stop, you look down to watch the rushing river that is flowing 200 feet below the bridge. Suddenly, from the woods comes a man holding a thick rope that is tied around his waist, he is running to you. "Catch," he yells as he throws the end of the rope in your direction.

Without thinking you catch the rope, and hold tight. The man then jumps over the edge of the bridge leaving you holding him in mid-air. There he stays, dangling 180 feet from certain death. It is up to you to keep him alive and you say, "Climb up, I can't hold for too much longer!" But the man does nothing.

After a few minutes, your palms start to sweat and the rope starts to slip. And you implore the man one more time, "Please, sir, climb! The rope is slipping." But the man does nothing. As your hands start cramping the rope finally gives way and the man plummets to his death. Just at that moment a lady comes walking down the bridge the other way and is shocked by what she just saw.

Who do you think she will blame for the man's death?

_____

_____

_____

Is this your fault?

_____

_____

_____

How do you think this relates to being a pastor? (After a few years in ministry you will feel like you are holding 15 ropes at one time.)

_____

_____

_____

So how do you combat being the one left holding the rope? Get others involved. Bring your wife with you when grieving women are involved and make it a habit to call wiser pastors. Too often it seems pastors are men who go running into the mess before they assess and then find themselves way over their head. (Remember, people mostly operate out of selfishness... they are not always telling the truth).

**3) Exodus 18:14-26**

_____

_____

_____

Delegate, delegate, delegate! This is the only thing that will save and expand your ministry.

Question: How do I determine which cases I should take care of myself and what to delegate?

**Level 1:** Do your best to delegate the person who says, "I just want a friend!" Remember, you don't have all the time in the world. Establish a friend's ministry for people who just want to talk (80% of problems are lonely people).

**Level 2:** Crisis moment, and it is obvious I need to engage the situation. When it is an issue of discipleship, deal with it by (1) developing trained people in your church who can disciple, but (2) for smaller churches or more serious issues, this may mean you are the only one who can help (includes issues of Abuse, Divorce, Pornography, and Addiction).

**Level 3:** They need professional help. Be willing to admit your main job is to teach the word, discipleship and prayer…you are not Sigmund Freud! How does Acts 6:1-7 illustrate this?

---------------------------------------------

---------------------------------------------

---------------------------------------------

Pastors are not super-heroes, we all need those people out there that have the expertise you need to lean on. Be humble and accept the help of others!

## Final Advice

The more you read, the more equipped you become. Here are some books that are necessary to help with issues of urgency:

- "Boundaries" By Henry Cloud (Issues dealing with healthy relationships)

- "When Love needs to be Tough" James Dobson (Issues dealing with marital abuse and estrangement)

- "Where is God when it Hurts" and "Disappointment with God" Philip Yancey (Issues of despair and doubt)

- "Reason for God" Tim Keller (Issues on forgiveness, love and existence)

Be a reader, and fill your soul so you will be more equipped when life is falling apart.

## GOD IS USING IT TO GROW YOU

Often, a crisis is used by God to make you a better pastor. When we are scared, God shows up. So wait on him, you don't need to be the hero, he is. God will often put you in situations that keep you humble, and then when he works through you glory alone will go to him. (See Psalm 115:1)

Memorize this: Lamentations 3:19-33, it is what ministry is all about!

Remember my affliction and my wanderings,
the wormwood and the gall!
My soul continually remembers it
and is bowed down within me.
But this I call to mind,
and therefore I have hope:
The steadfast love of the Lord never ceases
his mercies never come to an end;
they are new every morning;
great is your faithfulness.
"The Lord is my portion," says my soul,
"therefore I will hope in him."
The Lord is good to those who wait for him,
to the soul who seeks him.
It is good that one should wait quietly
for the salvation of the Lord.
It is good for a man that he bear
the yoke in his youth.
Let him sit alone in silence
when it is laid on him;
let him put his mouth in the dust–
there may yet be hope;
let him give his cheek to the one who strikes,
and let him be filled with insults.
For the Lord will not
cast off forever,
but, though he cause grief, he will have compassion
according to the abundance of his steadfast love;
for he does not afflict from his heart
or grieve the children of men.

# Final Encouragement

If you have tracked along through each week of this study I hope you have gained some clarity when it comes to having a calling from God on your life. The goal was to get you to think and wonder what is required to minister. It is time for you to be honest with yourself. Is this what you really want?

_____

_____

_____

_____

Put the following verses in your own words because this will become your job:

2 Corinthians 2:14-16

_____

_____

_____

2 Corinthians 4:7-14

_____

_____

_____

2 Corinthians 12:5-10

_____

_____

_____

So hopefully now you are ready to answer the final question: Are you "called"? If the answer is yes, remember. . .

"He who calls you is faithful; he will surely do it."
*1 Thessalonians 5:24*

For more ministry resources,
books and blogs visit:

www.christopherjweeks.com

www.ingramcontent.com/pod-product-compliance
Lightning Source LLC
Chambersburg PA
CBHW060337050426
42449CB00011B/2781